Everywhere Winds

pandemic haiku for the spirit

Alberto J. Montero

cover design by Tony Kellers

Print ISBN: 978-1-66783-1-701
eBook ISBN: 978-1-66783-1-718

For Marcela, Serg, and Gaby

"Whichever way the winds may blow, may they blow warm."

Cass McCombs

"Tell me what you feel about man,
and I shall tell you which art you cultivate."

José Ortega y Gasset

"My ambition is to say in ten sentences what everyone else
says in a book—what everyone else does not say in a book."

Friedrich Nietzsche

"En cada grano de arena hay
un derrumbamiento de montaña."

Dulce Maria Loynaz

EXISTENTIAL

Cleveland, OH

October, 2020

1

border walls won't save us

evil rides on everywhere winds

Pandora's hope torments

2

pandemic winds blow

treetops sway, and the forest moans

breathing in, she smells rain

3

our grief is a prism

colorless history transformed

iridescent fictions

4

winter: we pray for spring

but all resurrections require

Judas' ultimate kiss

5

crowned foe— small, yet mighty

shakes, sways, and quakes man's scaffolding:

microbial black swan

6

silent streets, empty shops

folk with yellow, blue masks reveal

plagued hearts and furrowed brows

7

patient's smell went on strike

after a stop the steal rally

now, smells death in COVID ward

8

nurses finish night shifts

with hospital-wearied faces

at dusk they will return

9

he can't breathe, coughs up blood

my primo's in the COVID-ward

his fear: a rotting corpse

10

she imagines her death—

a hole in her mask, a stray droplet:

doctor's pandemic toll

11

in our COVID dreams we've

all died in countless different ways—

always, same breathless end

12

their parents aren't numbers:

daughters who put on black dresses

weep at pandemic graves

13

a solemn red oak shades

mourners that are dressed in black from

the irreverent sun

14

death counts rising higher

with each COVID Greek letter wave—

pandemic trail of tears

15

ivermectin dreaming:

anti-vax zealots parading

in scientific robes

16

'Mask mandate is over!'

Gov declares over tacos, deaths

cruel Texas winds blow

17

twittercistic worship

#character isn't trending today—

look behind the curtain

18

MAGA flags on display

the blind demand blind eye justice

angry squall passes on

19

mad crescendo of lies

crass insurrection on Jan 6th

fragile democracy

20

our eyes are glass houses

I've got a slingshot for a heart

and rocks in both pockets

21

our plague fears keep rising

political fires stoke anger

with some breaths: tulips bloom

22

anger: toxic fuel

ego is a tiny matchbox

our desire lights the flame

23

lord vaccinate us now

against hatred and ignorance

inoculate our hearts

24

the unvaccinated—

behind ugly trumpian masks—

quietly hide their fears

25

Blues try whipping the ox—

forcing masks and vacs, but this just

makes folks resist the yoke

26

Reds resist health mandates

but freedom without duty is

a priest without the mass

27

her patient's dying now

husband's virtually bedside

his zoom tears sting her eyes

28

for Carol

patient's room: sacred space

I grieve for her; she comforts me

her strength: an orchid bloom

29

ICU doc wears herself down

her heart pierced by each COVID death

healer, heal yourself first

30

how can we mend ourselves?

this nation of jagged edges

red and blue, black, and white

ATMOSPHERIC

East Cleveland, OH

Feb, 2021

31

youths wear masks for others

they trade their freedoms for duties:

compassion's beating heart

32

serve one master—not two

that master is clearly not you

be compassion's axe

33

we create divisions:

ignorance and fear multiply

instead, sow compassion

34

blood binds us together

like wire. apparent differences—

imaginary lines

35

embrace fragility

remove your armor, lay down sword

accept life's slings, arrows

36

we hang hope on crosses

hiding raw truths behind plague masks:

simply, we are cast dice

37

we are spider and fly:

knowingly trapped in our own web

such fine shimmering threads

38

desire weaves many webs

attachment ensnares—spider's trap

exhale and cut the threads

39

the dreamer spins her thread

moonlight dances on dark waters

but who dreamt the dreamer?

40

desire is a small child

sit down with her, ask what she wants

rock her gently to sleep

41

then, now, after—borders?

empty mind, no separation

erase lines: the world blooms

42

water knows the way home

we resist, entangling ourselves

to sail, first lift anchor

43

roshi rings the bell twice.

sit. candle flames dance, incense drifts.

can you hear the silence?

44

we breathe in and then out

allowing our fears to move on

like an outgoing tide

45

we tremble in the now

floating on this fathomless sea:

a sea heart drift-, drift-- ing

46

wolf moon illuminates

fisherman searches in his skiff

winter sea holds her breath

47

blind girl at the beach knows

better than me about the sea

runs fingers through the waves

48

objects trapped in amber

desire's hungry ghost, haunts us all

but love is, noble glue

49

true love quenches ego

sacred primordial waters

no striving, just being

50

love sits above justice

and speaks not with words, but music:

flute, fiddle, and cymbal

51

love irreverently

right now, this moment, the present—

true flower of prophets

52

make your heart a mirror

courage, restraint, justice, wisdom

these virtues to reflect

53

take your thoughts for a walk

judgement stays home. wonder appears:

see again with child's eyes

54

thirsty self disappears:

a shimmering desert mirage.

you: a purposeless rose

55

no matter where you go—

remember, you can't shed your skin

—there you are, you are there

56

the truly heroic

distant from saccharine chatter

silence is its wellspring

57

the sculptor's hammer clangs

he speaks to this mountain rubble

and becomes chiseled stone

58

for my poems I cut

out skin and even bone until—

all that's left is marrow

59

lost in mid-life's vastness

I feel ancestral tides pulling

to Galician shores

60

Matt 16:26

a hollow victory—

world in your palm, yet lose your soul

sandcastles at high tide

SPIRIT CHASING

San Agustín

Dec, 2019

61

we become what we face

recognition—an afterthought

self: rides on formless winds

62

incense smoke meanders

nirvana finds the non-seeker

drawing from deep time's well

63

practice is the kindling

to make tea, you need a hot fire

empty hands know the way

64

language rings a cracked bell

drink from stillness's spring, which reaches

beyond words and logic

65

each breath, boundaries fade

cartesian distinctions topple

time becomes a lost child

66

our idea of 'me'—

just a cartesian house of cards

cast off like spoiled milk

67

thoughts cascading in, out

simple pleasures: stillness, breathing—

primordial silence

68

how subtle, the present—

unchanging and in constant flux:

ever flowing waters

69

quotidian silence

but in solitude's vast desert

God speaks in flaming tongues

70

there's a chaotic calm

in the eye of the hurricane

solemn as mossy trunks

71

rain taps on the skylight

but between the drip-drip of thoughts

in the emptiness: God

72

our prodigal shadows

disappear, like fickle children

when the sun shines brightest

73

we are more than, not just:

preferences, pronouns, possessions.

our roots hide in dark earth

74

sit. you become sitting.

just breathe. now you become breathing:

a lotus flower blooms

75

stillness, firmly rooted

every moment in constant flux

future casts long shadows

76

dawn holds the silence, night

lingers in our bodies. thoughts drift

like a kind candle flame

77

time is circle and line

cast off delusions like fall leaves

you are the warbler's song

78

crows caw, the wind replies

time is an empty-handed thief:

no beginning, no end

79

sound of the infinite—

not spoken word from ancient scrolls

it is the howling wind

80

no beginning, no end—

like some divine möbius strip

rising from time's ashes

81

taste eternity's cup

cultured men scoff, mystics tremble

time's obituary?

82

when we master our fears

will we still want eternal life?

ten thousand flowers bloom

83

Nietzsche's *challenge*

if we could relive in-

finitely all our joys, crosses

would we, nevertheless?

84

there's no ever after

why then all the hesitation?

take last shot, this is it

85

we do not live alone

all are petals from the same rose

we are candle and flame

86

what we can give away

like extravagant lovers

this I am thankful for

87

in our tranquility:

mental smoke of distinctions clears

outside: wind whips, rain drums

88

don't think about thinking

a thunderclap, smell of incense

you are that—your true self

89

we face the wall—breathe out

we cannot flee this life—breathe in

actualization

90

iron wall, silver peak

one way forward; no getting out

there it is; you are it

MYSTICAL

Cleveland

Little Italy

October, 2020

the earth quivers

her vibrations are a lullaby

you are a sieve

thoughts pass effortlessly through

flowing like sand

outside is a flaming bush

where Buddha is burning

his alms bowl

he chants you a question

asks which way to the soul

you point towards the universe

which trembles and groans at your accusation

a mirror provides the revelation

you stand there pointing at yourself